BLACK GIRL MAGIC
LIT MAG

ISSUE 3

TONYA JONES   MELODY KAY

NICOLE GIVENS KURTZ   ADRIENNE WALLACE

CERECE RENNIE MURPHY

Edited by KENESHA WILLIAMS
Edited by TIARA JANTE WIGFALL
Edited by KORTNEY HINTON

Dedicated to all the #ownvoices writers.

ACKNOWLEDGMENTS

Thank you as ever to my co-editors Tiara Jante and Kortney Hinton. You can read more about them here. http://www.blackgirlmagicmag.com/about-1/

Thank you for joining us on another magical ride for the third issue of *Black Girl Magic Lit Mag*.

As I reflected on submissions for the July issue, the now infamous speech by Jesse Williams given after he received his 2016 Humanitarian Award during the BET Awards kept running through my mind. The whole speech was brilliant and a much needed wake up call to Black America (and the world), but the part that stood out the most to me was him saying, "Just because we're magic doesn't mean we're not real".

It stuck out to me because in storytelling the trope of the *Magical Negro* is all too prevalent. The *Magical Negro* trope in fiction is when a Black character with some type of mystical powers, sometimes even God, is only in the story to function to help the white character to get their shit together and/or as a sacrificial lamb for the good of the white character(s). The *Magical Negro* usually has no story of their own, no family, and only serves as a way for a white character to learn a life lesson and transcend whatever character flaw they have to get the girl, win the fight, or whatever it is that good white main characters do.

The problem with the *Magical Negro* trope is threefold. First, the *Magical Negro* is only a plot device, they aren't a real character at all. Their only purpose is to help the white main character be less terrible. Secondly, the *Magical Negro* is the embodiment of the racist ideal of the "good Black", the *Magical Negro* is a one-dimensional and idolized figure and enforces the notion that there are certain categories of Black people and the *Magical Negro* is the exception in relation to other Black people. Lastly, the *Magical Negro* usually has a tragic end and for all it's supernatural otherness cannot save him or herself. Their power is only used for the good of the white main character.

What does that mean for Black people in real life? In real life we have doctors that somehow think that we feel less pain than our white counterparts because of some kind of supernatural powers we must all be imbued with at birth. Police officers fear us when we hold nothing in our hands and they have the full weight of the law and a 9mm in theirs. A study conducted by Adam Waytz of Northwestern University, Kelly Marie Hoffman, and Sophie Trawalter of the University of Virginia on this subject in *Social Psychological and Personality Science* April 2015 vol. 6 no. 3, entitled "A Superhumanization Bias in Whites' Perceptions of Blacks" came to the consensus that "long-held stereotypes about toughness, aggression, physicality, and sexuality" help to fuel the superhumanization that persists in the *Magical Negro* trope.

Here at *Black Girl Magic Lit Mag* we are reclaiming our magic because like Jesse said, not only are we magical, but we're also real. The stories we tell put us in the driver's seat. We use our magic to save ourselves, we are neither the victims nor the plot devices, we are the main character and we are in charge. Let us never forget that our magic is what makes us real. It is what has helped us endure the centuries of pain and subjugation on this continent and others throughout the world. We are both magic and real and we are the stars of our own stories.

I am happy to present to you our third issue with four original stories, one novel excerpt from a author Cerece Rennie Murphy, and an interview with Chanel Harry a horror author.

Thanks again for purchasing and we hope you enjoy!!!

Kenesha Williams
    Editor-in-Chief

I

FICTION

ZORA

TONYA JONES | 1283 WORDS

Everyone stared at me like I lost my mind. In one hand, I clutched my purse. With the other, I smoothed down my favorite purple dress. The one that snatched my curves. I checked to make sure the purple rose I put in my kinky hair was still in place. I know folks were looking at my face in disbelief. I had applied layers of shimmery eyeshadow and stained my lips a luscious berry. I heard someone say "umph" as I stopped in front of Zora's grave. I gave a slight shrug. Let these fools mourn Zora's life wearing all black and moaning goodbye songs. They know Zora would've laughed at them. But folks get weird about funerals. They think they have to do everything "respectably."

I cracked my gum, causing the same person to add on a couple more "umphs." I took Zora's gift out of my purse. I flipped the book to the first page. I pressed my lips against the paper leaving a perfect print. I bent down and placed the book on Zora's headstone. I gave a silent prayer and was gone. Within minutes, I was leaning against the hood of my car. I took a deep breath, as I watched folks shake their heads and continue on with the service. I fished around in my purse, wanting to crank up one of my e-cigarettes, but I know those things are bad for me. I found a Starburst. I flicked the tired gum out of my mouth and popped in the chewy candy. Ick, lemon, but it will do. I sucked the sour away as I thought about when I first met Zora.

It was the fall of 1988, my first day at Ida B. Wells High School. It was the first and last time I almost got into a fight.

"Whatcha' looking at?" the girl checked me as I walked down the hallway. I wasn't looking at anything. My head was down. It was the first day of 9th grade and I was mad I had to transfer to a new school. But mom thought I should be in a more "diverse" environment. "Hey! I'm talking to you!" I looked at the girl. She was tall, bony, and sporting finger waves. The girl would've been fly, except for the scowl on her face. She was standing with a group of girls. "Leave me alone." I said. "No, she didn't!" another girl said. The main girl wasn't about to be disrespected in front of her crew. "Whatcha' you say?" She jumped in my face. I didn't flinch. "Forget it. You aren't worth my time." I said. The girl was shocked. She reached over to knock my backpack off my shoulder. I pushed her hand away. The crew gasped. I could tell she didn't know how to respond. I saw her ball up her fist. I was ready though. I had taken karate at camp last summer. I got into a stance. "Yo, what she dong?" a third girl yelled in alarm.

"What's going on here?" Miss Davis, the assistant principal, suddenly appeared. I remembered her from the office when my mom registered me for this hood school. "Uh, nothing Miss Davis. We were just saying hi to the new girl." "Yes, sure. Everyone get to class. The bell will be ringing soon." The girl nodded at her crew. They strolled passed me. The bully gave me a dirty look. Miss Davis sighed and left. "You know Nia is going to be messing with your from now on, right?" A voice said behind me. I turned around. The cutest girl I ever saw in my life was standing near a row of lockers. I shrugged. "Dang, you always get into fights on the first day of school?" She laughed. "Don't start none, won't be none." I said. The cute girl looked me over. I felt uncomfortable under her gaze. I guess she decided there was something about me. "You're interesting." She said. I shrugged again.

"My name's Zora. What's yours?" "It's Toya." I said. I looked at her. "Zora? Like Zora Neale Hurston" I asked. "Yep. My mama likes her books." "Wow, how does your mom know about Zora?" I asked arrogantly. "What. You think 'hood' people illiterate? You sound as bad as white folks. We aren't ignorant, just surviving." Zora said. I felt shamed. "I meant--""Yeah, I know what you meant. You can't believe all that mess you see on TV." Zora wasn't mad, just amused by me. I decided I better get moving before she wanted to fight me too. "When do you have lunch?" Zora asked. I looked at her. "Uh, 4th period." "Dope. Me too. You want to eat together?" I didn't know what to say. "Let's meet here by the lockers at 12:30." Zora said. I nodded stupidly. I don't know why I agreed to do such a thing, but Zora had me hooked.

Zora looked at me. "You know, Nia's my cousin. I can tell her to leave you alone if you want." "That's okay. I'm not scared." Zora laughed. I liked her laugh. "Yeah, so I noticed. See you later." I watched her walk away. For some bizarre reason, Zora had me hooked. I liked her style. I wanted her puffy hair. I only saw women from my dad's old 70's movies wearing Afros. It framed her cute face perfectly. I wanted her walk. I watched as a boy tried to talk to her as she passed by him in the hall. Zora winked and he tripped over his feet. I smiled. Zora would be my best friend from that day on.

I licked at the salty tears. We had been best friends for over twenty years. Even after I went away to college, got married, then divorced. Zora stayed in the community to go to school and do her activist work. I remembered the sweet kisses we shared and how we would snuggle close in bed. Or hold hands as we strolled around the mall. We had a sister girl love. Zora had fallen off a ladder while hanging a banner for a neighborhood fundraiser. She broke her neck, instantly. "Oh no, not you too." Zora said. I looked to my side and saw Zora's ghost relaxing next to me. A couple of nights ago, the ghost appeared in my living groom. I'd been gulping down glasses of wine to prepare for the funeral. I knew I had to be drunk, when I saw her winking at me. But when she showed up the next morning and the following night, I decided to roll with it. She had did most of the talking. I had promised not to cry.

"You got anymore Starburst?" Zora asked. I unwrapped a cherry candy and handed it to her. I watched as the candy dissolved in her mouth. Why didn't it fall to the ground? I tried to remember ghost movies I had seen. "What am I going to do without you?" I asked. Zora gave me a look. "You are going to keep on doing you." She said. Suddenly, I felt tired. Zora looked towards the sky. "My time is up. You promised you wouldn't cry." I shrugged. "You know I hate when you do that." Zora smiled. "I love you." I felt something brush against my face. "I love you too." I watched as she merged into the clouds. I stood there for a few minutes, then got into my car. I dangled my hand out the window. A stream of sunlight played with my fingers until it faded away. I sighed. I guess I was going to be alright.

To read more about this author visit the Author Spotlight.

DO OVER

MELODY KAY | 5272 WORDS

Kimberly elbowed her way through the large group of chiffon-clad bridesmaids. Her light brown skin and natural hair made her stand out amongst the cluster of white women. They were the groom's obnoxious family and Kimberly had had enough.

She pushed to the front of the impatient crowd and was met with a closed door. Kimberly tapped her knuckles against the wood, then she entered the small upper room. She immediately spotted her best-friend on the floor in her strapless wedding gown with a glass bottle of Merlot in her hands. The bride was sitting in the corner. Her knees were drawn up and her eyes were turned up too at the open window above her. Kimberly settled next to her on the floor and crossed her legs.

"What are we looking at?"

"The sky," said Faith. "It's so blue."

It was quite blue. Cerulean blue. The sky was as beautiful as it was endless.

"It's the worst day of my life and the sky?"

Faith pressed her chin to her collarbone and looked into the wine bottle. Shiny black ring curls fell over her bare golden brown shoulders.

"There isn't a cloud in the sky," Faith said.

She raised the bottle to her red lips and drank more wine. She drank and drank until Kimberly reached over and put her fingertips on the butt of bottle to gently push it down.

"You came, you saw, the same thing happened. Let's go home," said Kimberly.

Faith shook her head and sniffled. "One more time."

"Jesus Christ."

"This is the last one. I promise."

Kimberly and Faith locked eyes. The promise and luster of the day wore off hours ago. All that remained in the bride's dressing room were two tired 29-year-old black women putting wrinkles in their expensive dresses.

"Alright," said Kimberly with a long, heavy sigh.

"Thank you."

They stood up and went to the vanity. Faith put the wine bottle down on the floor and grabbed a tissue to dry the runny makeup on her cheeks. Flowers, square shaped perfume bottles, makeup brushes, and hair accessories were scattered over the counter. Close to the edge of the vanity there was a metal hot comb with charcoal black teeth and a honey colored handle. Kimberly picked it up and pointed it at the mirror.

The glass rippled like water before it became foggy.

"I went first last time," said Kimberly glancing at Faith.

Faith knocked everything off the vanity with one giant sweep of her arms. Then she hitched up her gown and put one knee on top of the counter. Hesitant, she reached one arm into the mirror and the fog faded away. The glass became dark. Kimberly took a step backwards. Faith held her breath and climbed into the world behind the mirror. Once she'd disappeared, Kimberly took a look around the room one more time.

Then Kimberly held her breath and leapt inside behind Faith.

Aaron grabbed Faith around the waist and gave her a tight hug.

His arms encircled her and it felt so good to be held after not being held by anyone for such a long time. His chest was pressed against her chest, his stomach against her stomach. They pulled apart slowly. Faith brushed her cheek against his cheek. He smelled good. Like freshly cut wood and perfumed smoke. Masculine and strong. His dark stubble tickled her soft skin.

An airplane roared overhead and rattled the objects around them. The stars were out. Blue lights from O'Hare International created a glittering haze of urgency. They didn't flash or anything but they might as well have been police lights. It was time to let go and Faith knew it, but she didn't want to. She wanted more time with Aaron. She wanted to be held a little longer. Talk more. Drink more. Even though she wanted it all she would've settled for whatever she could get. She would have settled for just one kiss.

So she pulled back in slow motion almost. They looked into each other's eyes. He patted her back, his palm open and flat, and then he let her go.

"Thanks for everything," he said.

Aaron picked up his duffle bag and slipped the strap on his shoulder.

Her body missed the warmth of his chest and stomach.

"Take care of yourself."

"Yeah, you too," she said.

She forced a smile and he waved as he turned his back on her. He walked inside O'Hare International. Faith went to her car and lowered herself inside the driver's seat.

But she took one more backwards glance. The back of his shirt and the shape of his head formed in her long-term memory. It pressed against her mind and left an imprint, his unique mark, and it never went away.

As soon as Faith recalled the memory, she knew that that was the one. The last road they hadn't gone down.

Standing in a vast room with a solid floor and no ceiling, Kimberly watched the clock tower in the middle. It had a gleaming white face and roman numerals. Behind it and all around it was an infinite deep purple galaxy. Blue bands of stars arched between hundreds of planets like the Milky Way. Except the planets weren't planets. They were rectangle shaped mirrors of every size and decoration. They floated all around, suspended by magic.

The mirrors hovering the closest to the clock tower were black. Solid black. The glass had been painted over with tar.

Kimberly ignored everything except the time on the clock. She folded her arms and tapped the end of the hot comb against her chin absentmindedly as she watched the second hand and the minute hand move counter clockwise.

Tock.

Tick.

Tock.

Tick.

Her dress transformed back into a t-shirt and jeans when she crossed over, the outfit she left home in. Kimberly's fluffy natural hair was tied back with a headband. She reached up and almost scratched the top of her head with the hot comb and then stopped herself.

"I found it," Faith called to Kimberly.

"Hurry up and pull it down. We only have a few more minutes."

Faith stood several feet away from the clock in a sun dress and platform sandals. She looked up at a full-length mirror with a simple red frame. No embellishments. Nothing fancy. She squatted and leapt into the air. Faith grabbed it by its corner and yanked her arm down.

The mirror hit the floor and bounced two times before it settled.

In the glass, Faith didn't see her reflection. Instead she saw the moment she was thinking of with Aaron. It was something akin to a video of their hug at the airport. The moment was playing on repeat in the glass. That hug was the last time she ever touched him. The airport was the last time she ever saw him.

"This is it. This one's gonna be the one," said Faith. "Let's do it."

Kimberly sighed and walked away from the clock. It kept moving in reverse.

"We're not doing another one. I mean it. This is it for real."

She held out the hot comb and felt it shake in her hands when the smooth glass surface changed into liquid. The glass turned black.

It was Kimberly's turn to go first.

"Take care of yourself," Aaron said to Faith.

Kimberly watched from a distance on a bench outside the airport. The crush of cars, buses, and shuttles were thinning out. She had her luggage nearby and a bag in her lap. Kimberly put the hot comb inside and zipped it shut.

Aaron waved and turned away from Faith.

Kimberly felt her stomach clench. Her blood pressure was rising.

"Wait."

Aaron turned around and raised his eyebrows. Unlike last time Faith didn't let him leave. She closed the gap between them, threw her arms around his neck and kissed him. He stumbled backwards a little and then found his footing. He dropped his bag and wrapped her up in his arms again.

Unlike last time Faith didn't let him get away.

Midnight came and Faith didn't sleep because she wanted to admire Aaron's porcelain skin a little bit longer. His muscles were relaxed and his dark brown eyes were looking at her dark brown eyes.

He asked, "How'd you know?"

Faith shifted onto her side. She ran her hand through her black hair. "How did I know what?"

"How'd you know to stop me?"

She frowned a little and then laughed softly. She knew because she'd jumped through eight other mirrors before she came to this one. Eight different lifetimes were lived. Eight different hypothesis' tested. Eight different starting points and ending dates. This was the only one she hadn't tried yet. This was the only timeline she hadn't touched and it could be the only alternative universe where Aaron didn't leave her. Faith was here to find out.

She finally replied, "Ummmm... I didn't."

"I wanted to kiss you. I was going to."

Faith laughed again and nodded. "Sure you were."

"I get kinda shy about stuff like that."

"Me too."

He reached out for her and she leaned in to kiss him again.

K imberly sat patiently in the hotel lobby. She drank coffee quietly as she watched Aaron and Faith leave the elevator hand-in-hand. They were glowing. Her bags were beside her and the one with the hot comb in it vibrated when Aaron and Faith walked past her on their way out of the door.

Briefly, very briefly, Faith made eye contact with Kimberly. Then they went back to ignoring each other. Kimberly had to keep an eye on them. It was her job. They couldn't stay in this alternative universe forever. When it was time to go, Kimberly was the one who had to open the portal... and the one who had to drag Faith away. There was no mirror world in the entire galaxy equipped to hold them for all of eternity. Masquerades always ended eventually. Faith knew that too.

Once they were out of sight, Kimberly picked up her bags and saw them get back into Faith's car in the parking lot.

Kimberly didn't want to admit it but this was a path they really hadn't explored. She was convinced that the two of them making out in the car was the furthest Faith would ever get on this road. She was wrong. Their passionate petting led to the hotel and to Aaron missing his flight, but by the looks on their faces Kimberly could tell they were pleased by this turn of events.

She wasn't.

She waved down a cab. A driver appeared a few seconds later in front of the hotel.

"Where ya goin?"

"To the airport."

The driver nodded and Kimberly tossed her bags into the backseat. She eased inside and slammed the door shut.

F aith kept as still and quiet as humanly possible. She waited. And waited.

Aaron and his friends were laughing in the other room and she couldn't wait any longer. She waded into the waters of eight other universes for a moment like this and she'd be a fool to miss it.

"Yeah, I guess I gotta do it big since I'm - "

The door cracked open and the guys stopped talking. Aaron turned around and his mouth fell open.

Faith emerged from the room. She was dressed like a pin-up girl from another era. Her halter dress adorned her every curve. Her high heeled pumps were perfect. Her hair was styled into a trendy bob with shiny bangs. She'd spent hours preparing her eyeliner and red matte lipstick.

"Happy birthday to you," she sang as she crossed the room. Aaron's friends grinned at them. One took out his phone and started filming. "Happy birthday to you. Happy birthday, Mr. President, happy birthday..."

She put her arms around Aaron, he held her hips, they smiled and gazed into each other's eyes.

"... to you."

"I, uh, I think I'm gonna call it a night," Aaron said to his friends.

They all laughed.

This didn't happen in the other mirrors. Faith had never seen these things or heard these words and it made her heart swell with joy and hope.

The clock tower in the blue and purple galaxy began turning clockwise.

All of the mirrors around it shook. The stars flickered and the colors wavered.

The universes were intertwined and time only moved backwards to document new events that had never happened before. They were the beginnings of new time-lines, their starting points taken from reality. When the alternate universes converged, like they always did and would always do, the clock couldn't go backwards anymore. The red mirror was still on the floor. It was the only mirror on the floor and the color of the frame was beginning to change too from red to black. New to old. The light in the glass was dimming. The reflection was becoming grainy, dirty, hard to see through and hard to see in.

The clock tower kept turning, this time in the right direction.

Tick.

Tock.

Tick.

Tock.

Kimberly swore she could feel the whiskey swishing in her stomach and the Fireball still burning her throat even though that was an hour ago. All around her were party goers and drug addicts. Young people of all races and colors, from all walks of life.

She stumbled her way off the dance floor, away from the sweaty bodies and hands of men she didn't know. It was hot under those strobe lights. Kimberly took a big refreshing breath of cool air and ripped a neon green glow stick necklace off her body. Her clothes and her curly hair were damp. It was sticking to her face, her back, her arms and legs.

Kimberly thought to herself in a lightheaded, drunken daze, 'Where is Faith?'

A small sign pointing towards the rest area turned on a light-bulb in Kimberly's head. She made her way to the toilets immediately. The thumping bass from the electronica songs weren't as loud in the bathroom. The pulsating sounds were somewhat muted.

Kimberly looked underneath the first few stalls for Faith's feet and then felt like she was going to vomit. She went back to the sinks. The nausea passed. She groaned and closed her eyes. A woosh of fresh air came in behind her when the door opened and Faith came up to her.

She hugged Kimberly from behind and laughed.

"This is it," Faith told Kimberly. "I know it. I know for sure this time that this is it."

"You thought the last five mirrors were the one too."
Kimberly grinned.

Then she turned around and came face-to-face with a
dazzling engagement ring.

"It's happening!"

Faith held her hand up with pride and excitement. She
drank in the confidence and the sense of accomplishment
that came from having a man put such a ring on one's finger.

"You got engaged in the last universe, remember?"
Kimberly said.

"But now I did it twice. He proposed to me twice and it
wasn't the same this time. It was better. It was more romantic, more sexy, surprising." Faith smiled. "I told you this is
the one."

"Okay. Good for you. You figured it out. Now that we've
seen what could've been, can we go back home?" Kimberly
asked.

"Let me see it through to the wedding," said Faith.

Kimberly tossed her head back and groaned as loud as
she could.

"Please, Kim."

"Fine."

Faith hugged Kimberly. She didn't hug her back.
Kimberly's arms were left limp at her sides as Faith
teared up.

"I'm so happy," she said. "And it's all because of you.
Thank you."

She pulled back and looked at the ring again. Faith squealed, winked at Kimberly and ran out of the bathroom. The intensity of the bass and the noise pollution seeped inside for a moment until the door shut again.

Kimberly gripped the sink with both hands and looked at herself in the mirror. She looked as inebriated as she felt.

'What if this is the one?' She thought. 'What if she cracked the code?'

It would change everything Kimberly believed about the layout of the universe. Ever since she was a child her mother and her grandmother told her stories about the alternative universes. Kimberly remembered sitting at her grandmother's feet next to the stove as she talked and talked and pressed her hair with the hot comb. Back then it wasn't science that turned her tight, unruly curls into 'white girl hair' -- it was magic.

That magic extended far beyond the physical, as her mother always said. There was only one rule in the galaxy and it was a rule that Kimberly had never broken herself and had never seen someone else break either.

What's meant to happen is going to happen and there's nothing anyone can do about it.

The different mirror worlds didn't exist to change the present. They were exactly what they looked like: mirrors. They were reflections of the black woman. The mirrors showed them what they wanted to see for a little while. And because the universe loved them, it entertained their most fantastic fantasies. The mirrors were windows into what could've been but they never changed what really was. Kimberly couldn't help but wonder... had Faith found a way around that? Did Faith break the mirror?

In no other universe had Kimberly ever gotten this drunk or felt this discouraged.

"I hope she's wrong," she whispered to herself.

Kimberly turned on the faucet, splashed water on her face, and stumbled back to the dance floor.

————

The hands on the clock slowed down.

Tick...

Tock...

They were persistent in moving forward until now.

Tick..

Tock..

The clock stopped and a mighty bell rang. The mirrors trembled and then they stopped too.

Everything stopped.

————

They were meeting in one of the larger parks in Chicago where the most vibrant colors of fall were all around them. Crisp yellows and faded oranges and so many shades of red dotted the trees and lined the horizon. Kimberly sat on a park bench on her laptop wrapped up in a thick scarf and jacket. She glanced up every now and then at Aaron and Faith. They were having a lively conversation under a gazebo.

Faith's journey and her relentless pursuit of Aaron across the cosmos was the love story she didn't know she wanted. Even after she sobered up and realized that Faith was high on her own euphoria, Kimberly was curious. What kind of man was destined to be in her life? What kind of relationship would the universe eventually create for her? Was there someone out there that she was meant to be with? Was there someone out there that would travel through time and space just for her?

After all, like Faith, she was almost 30. And she was single too.

Her contemplative questions brought her to a lifestyle website for black women. She did a search for 'married.' The first headline that appeared made her smile.

I'm a Single Black Girl and I Refuse To Be Scared By The Statistics Saying I Will Never Get Married

She clicked on the article and inhaled the words. The encouragement and optimism filled her veins. Kimberly silently thanked the writer and glanced up in enough time to see Faith and Aaron step out of the gazebo to meet their engagement photographer.

Kimberly gasped.

From where she was sitting, she could only see the back of the woman's head and it was full of wavy brown hair. Aaron looked relaxed and calm. Faith's smile faltered and she recovered as fast as she could.

"Oh no," said Kimberly. She closed her laptop and leapt from the bench.

R iya.

Faith couldn't get the name out of her head. Aaron couldn't stop talking about her.

"Her work is amazing," he said looking through her portfolio website at the table. They were grabbing lunch at a little cafe before heading home.

Faith knew Riya was amazing. She was an incredible photographer. She used to work for the New York Times. She won awards. She was talented and gifted.

"One of my friends from work told me about her so I didn't really look her up before hand."

Mutual friends introduced them in every timeline. In eight alternative universes, not including real-life, Riya found her way to Aaron through a mutual friend who told him about her. The fact that that detail hadn't changed in eight timelines was astonishing to Faith.

"You like her, right?"

No. Faith did not like her. She hated her. She despised

Riya and everything she was and everything she'd done across the galaxies.

"Yeah," she said to Aaron, faking a big smile. "I like her."

A bell jingled over the door to the cafe and Faith glanced up to see Kimberly easing inside. She settled down at a table, ordered and then went to the bathroom.

"I'll be right back. I want to wash my hands," Faith said.

Aaron smiled, "Okay, babe."

She took her time walking to the bathroom, but once she finally got inside she burst into tears. Kimberly hugged her and Faith sobbed.

"I'm so sorry," said Kimberly. "Let's get out of here."

"No."

"You know what's going to happen," said Kimberly.

"I can't," Faith said. She pulled back and wiped her eyes. "This time it's not her. It's me. This time it's supposed to be me."

Kimberly sighed. "The same thing is going to happen."

"No." Faith shook her head. "You don't know that for sure. This time has been so different."

"And now Riya's here. Again. It's not different, Faith."

"But - "

"Listen to me." Kimberly softened her tone of voice. "It's time to go home. It's time to let go."

Faith turned away from Kimberly and grabbed some hand napkins. She dried her face in the mirror and dabbed at her eye makeup.

When she was done, she took a deep breath and headed towards the bathroom door.

"Don't do this to yourself," Kimberly said gently.

She paused, looked over her shoulder at Kimberly and lowered her head. She opened the door and went back into the cafe.

The first alternative universe ended before it began. Aaron boarded his flight at O'Hare International. Faith was aggressive with her phone calls and her texts and her video chats. She'd always believed Aaron gave up on her and got together with Riya because she didn't make herself clear. She didn't let him know right away how much she liked him and how much she cared. He was turned off by it all and that was the end of that.

The second alternative universe was extremely different. Aaron and Faith never made it to the airport. She told him at the bar that she enjoyed her time with him that day. They made out a little bit. He bought them another round of drinks. Faith was too drunk to drive so Aaron bought her a cab and then took one himself. For a few weeks they tried to make plans to see each other again. Then Faith got frustrated and angry. It took days to get him on the phone.

"Why does it feel like I'm the only one putting in all the effort?"

They exchanged emails and then Faith got frustrated again. Aaron slowly faded out of her life. One day she opened Facebook and saw the engagement picture. Top of the page. Hundreds of 'likes'. He called Riya the best thing that ever happened to him.

The third universe was a lot like the real-life version. Aaron and Faith tried to keep the fire alive. But there was too many circumstances pulling them apart. Distance, money, time.

The fourth universe was devastating for Faith. They had sex. A quick encounter in a dark corner of the airport parking garage. Faith had always wondered what it was like to be intimate with Aaron up until that point. She figured she might as well try it and see what happened. She usually never did things like that. She hoped her boldness would pay off and create a different outcome. Sex could help her. It worked for other women who put out on the first date, so why not her?

Ironically, Aaron never spoke to her again after he boarded that plane. Kimberly did some digging and discovered in that universe Aaron thought she wasn't very respectable for "throwing herself" at him like that.

He thought Faith was "classier" than that.

Kimberly knew they were pushing the boundaries of both the real world and the mirror world when Faith insisted that they dip their toes into the fifth alternative. She called it off before Aaron could. She thought Aaron would try to keep things going if she were the one who dumped him instead of the other way around.

He only married Riya faster.

In the sixth universe, Faith tried to break up Aaron and Riya. It didn't work.

In the seventh universe, Riya broke up Aaron and Faith. Faith was livid.

Then the eight universe came and Riya didn't appear until after everyone had set the date on their calendars and bought their wedding gifts and attended the rehearsal dinner. Faith was certain that this time she could prove that under the right circumstances Aaron would be hers.

He left her at the altar for Riya on beautiful sunny day. Now Faith was almost nine losses out of nine.

It ate her up inside.

It destroyed her.

T he weather was perfect spring weather.

Faith and Aaron sat on a patio outside a bar. It was late. On a weekday. Not at all crowded but not empty either. She sat back in her seat and smiled at him. He smiled back. For a while they sat in silence with their beers between them.

No one said anything.

They smiled and enjoyed the peace and quiet.

Faith was thinking about the real events and the real trajectory of everything that didn't happen with Aaron. The way he smiled at her, his kindness, his friendship. However, she couldn't ignore the bad.

She was starving and he always gave her a taste when she wanted the whole entree. He could only give her so much, he said, because he was busy. She was always in a state of longing and missing and wanting. It was a miserable way to live. Being perpetually unsatisfied was no way for a beautiful young black woman to live.

In real-life he was only passing the time with her. The way he called when he was bored and rarely showed any interest in her personal life, should've been red flags. Big red flags.

He moved on immediately. He moved on so fast from her, Faith couldn't believe it. He removed her from his 'rotation' as if she were an object. It hurt. It made her insecure. It made her hate herself. It made her wonder if she hadn't pressured him for a proper ending, then he would've been perfectly fine without saying goodbye. Faith was not the kind of person to love someone and then walk away without saying goodbye. She couldn't love someone who could leave her without saying goodbye.

Then there was the one thing that hurt Faith the most. The one she didn't want to believe was true.

Aaron didn't feel the same way about her.

Faith didn't want to accept what was right in front of her face. He didn't owe her a ring after X amount of time together. A breakup wasn't a democratic decision, so when she demanded a proper goodbye, he was well within his rights to deny. She wished she could make him return her feelings. She felt she deserved a relationship. She felt wronged. But she hadn't been wronged. He hadn't wronged her at all.

Faith and Kimberly watched from the shadows across the street as Riya and Aaron settled down at a table in a trendy restaurant. The city lights cast long shadows over some things and left others in complete darkness.

They smiled shyly at each other as Aaron's official love affair with Riya began. Again. Faith knew what was going to happen next. Kimberly was right. She didn't have to do this to herself and she didn't have to stick around and get her heart broken for the tenth time.

"Let's get out of here," said Kimberly.

Kimberly reached through the mirror, her hands coming out first, then her head and her body. She stepped through onto the floor and inhaled.

"Ow," said Faith as she tripped on the frame and tumbled inside the galaxy.

Kimberly helped her to her feet.

"That whole universe hates me so much it shoved me on the way out," she said, dusting herself off.

"That's not true," said Kimberly. "The universe loves us."

Exasperated, Faith rolled her eyes and waved her hand.

They watched as the glass in the mirror turned black. The frame faded slowly to gray and then dark gray and then finally another shade of black. It floated back up to its original space in the sky and stayed there. The world inside was locked and frozen. Never to be explored again.

They walked over to the base of the clock tower. Their heads turned up as they looked at the clock moving in reverse again, the hands running counter clockwise.

Faith bit her lip and tried not to cry, but the emotions had been building up inside of her for hours. She'd stacked her pain and confusion on top of each other and now they were bleeding together. The dam was breaking.

"If she's meant for him and he's meant for her, then who's meant for me?"

Kimberly glanced at Faith as the stars twinkled around them.

"You just haven't met him yet," said Kimberly. She raised her arms to the sky. "He's out there in the galaxy."

Faith cried into her hands. "But why?"

"Why isn't he here yet?" Kimberly asked.

"Why do I have to wait when other girls don't?" Faith wept.

"I don't know." Kimberly walked over to a mirror with a silver frame made from metal. "Your life path is different, as we just confirmed nine times. It doesn't have to be a bad thing."

"They were meant to happen. They were so meant to be that nothing could come between them. I'm the thing that couldn't come between them."

"You're not a thing."

Kimberly reached up and tugged the mirror down. It fell slowly and bounced when it hit the ground.

"I'm a footnote in their relationship." Faith tried to compose herself and wipe her eyes. "I feel like a fool."

"It happened and now it's over," said Kimberly. She pulled the hot comb from her back pocket.

"That's it? That's all you have to say?"

Kimberly smiled and turned to face Faith as she walked over to the mirror.

"They're background characters in your story. Listen. You're not a fool or a thing standing between them. Girl, forget them. From now on, their footnotes in your galaxy."

The hot comb sent a ripple across the glass.

Faith rubbed her eyes and her nose and tried to smile at Kimberly.

They walked through the mirror and the clock stopped. The stars turned off and the colors faded away. All that remained was the deep purple sky and the mirror turning back into the mirror.

To read more about this author visit the Author Spotlight.

SUNSHINE

NICOLE GIVENS KURTZ | 2400 WORDS

> "Keep your face to the sunshine and you cannot see a shadow."
> --Helen Keller

Warmth burrowed through her thick blanket of sleep. It didn't ask permission for entry, but instead pushed aside slumber's all-encompassing hold, wrenching Geraldine into reality's harsh and cold embrace with complete indifference. A straight-up betrayal of the sun's promise to keep her warm.

Rude.

Geraldine rubbed her eyes and winced against the room's brightness. For most, sunlight meant life. Plants created food from it and people survived on their output, oxygen and food.

But for an unlucky few, the sun meant death.

As if demons could ever truly die. Geraldine pushed the thought aside, as she sat up, and nudged her tabby, Katrina, to the floor. Kat responded with an angry meow.

"I don't wanna be awake either." Geraldine pushed her dreadlocks back from her face.

Nevertheless, she was awake. Golden sunlight poured through the parted blinds and into her private space. She stretched out her hands and touched a ray, twisting it in her fingertips as she pulled from the magic within herself. As she did so, the room's walls dissolved into bright light before reforming as the corner of the institution's stone block walls. From the blinds, the sun's rays shimmered and cast strange patterns across the hardwood floor and Geraldine's yellow bedding. Illuminated dust danced in the air and mixed with the heady scent of magic.

...and sulfur.

Demons.

She rolled out of bed, stretched, and tied her locks into a bun at the base of her neck. With her hands on full hips, she called out.

"Speak. I know you're here."

The shadows bulged and burst. A sizzling grew louder as a form solidified into a hazy silhouette.

Geraldine shook her head. "You demons suck at mimicking."

The shadow flickered and tightened into more of a human outline, forming a face with eyeless sockets.

"Come on all damn ready. It's too early for this." Geraldine folded her arms and waited.

"Come. On. Geee." The huddled form's face split into a gaping mouth. Its voice mocked her in a travesty of antiquated urban slang.

"That's how you show respect? Get out. I'm going back to bed."

Without waiting to see if the entity complied, she climbed back into bed and waited. Kat co-signed on this course of action, and leapt back onto the bed. She started kneading the covers, purring in anticipation, and prepping for another nap.

"Must you be cruel?" The echoing wheeze of their words filled the room.

Their voice made Geraldine's skin crawl. A thousand souls crushed in agony and amplified as one. She hated that they'd come to visit her--again. Each time attempting to provoke her into doing the one thing that would grant them pleasure--her death.

They wouldn't kill her. No, that wouldn't be nearly as satisfying as watching her mental torment and then in glee, witnessing her taking her own life. Demons envied humans of her lineage, and wanted her to be among them. A certain ticket she'd end up in Hell, with them.

"Cruelty and honesty are hard to distinguish from each

other, especially for your kind." She fluffed her pillow, and turned back to face them.

"Our kind is your kind." Their arms gestured to her and then dissolved into the huddle form again.

Geraldine quirked an eyebrow at the comment. Rumors from her family had hinted at their lineage and part of the source of their power coming from an evil source. She didn't believe it. Her momma hailed from a land drenched in the sun's power. They harnessed the universe's magic, the power from a star. Now, she did too. Despite the golden orb's reluctance, she would pool the sunlight into power. Her momma spoke of how the sun despised being under their yoke, so it burned their flesh when they tried to absorb too much. When her skin captured its energy, she used it to ignite the magic inside her.

Geraldine sighed. Demons. Didn't they have other things to do? With her palms raised, she called upon the cells in her body to conjure the magic in preparation for their possible attack. As she focused, her skin began to tingle.

The demons' poorly contrived physical presence shimmered in her bedroom's early morning glow. The situation must be dire for them to contact her during the day, when the sun was up.

"What do you want?" Geraldine repeated.

They wouldn't leave unless she at least allowed them to tempt her. That's the rule of how she ended up in this place, summoning demons to strengthen her own inherit powers had caused her to kill her best friend. Geraldine spoke to the lawyers that the demons had tricked her, and now, she resided here. Each day, they came to try again.

Once she'd done that, she'd send them back to the cozy lake of fire they slipped out from. Maybe then, she'd get some sleep.

"We have a surprise for you." The demons declared.

"What?" Geraldine asked, but as soon as she did, three hard knocks burrowed through the door seconds before two large men, dressed in white, button-down shirts, and matching pants rushed into the room.

"Why even bother knocking?" She said. Not this again. She turned to the demons. "You guys lack originality."

"Who you talkin' to? On the mattress, Gerry!" Matthew, one of the orderlies, slammed his fist against the wall. "Or it's back to the padded room."

"Geraldine! My name's Geraldine!"

She balled up her fists, the hairs on her neck standing in rapt attention. Beside her, Kat vanished into the sunlight's glow. The small rectangular room, narrow, and similar to other rooms in the institution, held everything she loved. Those things now dissolved into the sunlight.

With each step Matthew took, the blinds, the comfortable bedding--all vanished, leaving only an iron-wrought bedframe, thin mattress with scratchy sheets and threadbare rug.

Geraldine fought to slow her breathing and to retain

control as she slid out from her bed, watching the orderlies, Matthew in particular.

"What did I do this time?" The demons had sent them.

When she looked over to the mass of darkness masquerading as a person, she found them watching with rapt attention. Or so she imagined, since their concealed form had no facial features.

"It don't matter what you done or didn't do. You gonna do what I say." Matthew marched further into her personal space.

"No." The word came out in calm enunciated syllable.

"No?" He folded his arms and smirked. "You what they call mentally ill, Gerry. Fucking crazy. You do what I tell you."

Danger gleams like sunshine to a brave man's eyes.

Euripides' words echoed in Geraldine's mind as she watched the two men prepare to attack. Although dressed in white, their souls were stained with streaks of filth. They had been tasked with maintaining order in the institution. As if. They could barely handle breathing and walking at the same time.

She readied herself for the familiar game. Despite the seriousness of the situation, it was a game, a match between herself and the darkness, the demons.

"Aye, look, man, she got that wild stare again. Let's go." Rod, the other orderly, tugged on Matthew's shirt before he backed out of the room.

Geraldine could smell his acidic sweat--an indicator of

his terror. He made a feeble attempt to take Matthew with him, but the larger, orderly shook him off.

"Coward. We gotta job to do," Matthew said over his shoulder.

Geraldine felt the oily demonic creep further into her room. Demons had life eating powers. Drawn entirely by instinct, the spirits' vast and potent nature fed on human misery. None were more miserable than those in an insane asylum. The more emotional, the more horrific. The roar of the collective outrage of the deranged, the depraved, and the depressed, echoed through her opened door. She understood why they came to torment her.

"Besides, she's a piece of shit head case." Matthew leered, his own fists drawn tight.

"It ain't right." Rod's voice quivered like a kite caught in a hell storm.

Rod and Matthew had become a sadistic show in constant replay. The bruising from their last round of "fun" hadn't yet changed into the sickening dark green of healing along her legs and arms.

Matthew snatched Rod's shirt into one of his large fists. Rod tried unsuccessfully to dislodge it. They scuffled, their voices descending into grunts and grumblings before dissolving into a thousand souls crushed into one.

Demons.

"Get out!" Matthew shoved Rod with one hard push and sent him windmilling out into the hallway.

Just as Rod regained his footing, Matthew slammed the door closed.

Geraldine's skin felt cold so she turned to the warmth. When she reached toward the sun, her fingers brushed the rays and she felt instant joy.

She giggled.

"The hell you laughin' at bitch?" Matthew jerked his shirt down where it had crept over his belly.

Geraldine ignored the buzzing noise, the sound of the demons' attempts to sync together, and Matthew. The sun's waves held much more promise than the dark shadow huddling inside her room, dressed in a white orderly uniform. The burning star offered power, hope, and above all freedom.

Wham! The blow against her neck ignited a flare of pain and sent her crashing to the bed. The springs of the lumpy mattress hid just beneath the threadbare fabric. One of them scraped her cheek, drawing blood. With her cheek on fire and her back in agony, Geraldine had scarcely a moment to breathe, before Matthew continued his assault by punching her in the back, slamming his fist into her kidney.

Geraldine didn't cry out. The days of screaming for a rescue, for a change, for someone in the institution to acknowledge the depravity that visited her room, had faded like the room's sun-bleached wallpaper. In those earlier dark years, when her screams had littered the corridors, the ceilings, and the walls, along with her spilled blood, through the fog of agony, a becaon had shone. Her power erupted and she learned to use it.

Unafraid, Geraldine rolled off the bed, using the momentum Matthew had unleashed to her advantage. Now, she had room to work. Breathing through the pain, she called upon her solar magic.

After all, she was made of stars.

The morning's sunlight streamed behind her, warming her back, her neck, and her hair, giving her strength despite her injuries as it did so. The sun poured its power into her, illuminating her, bringing her magic to her fingertips. She stood tall as she raised her palms to face him.

"Leave my space or face my fury."

His smudge of a face, blurred now as the demons' control over Matthew broke down, smiled.

"I ain't leavin'. This stinkin' place reeks of your people's stink."

"That's brimstone and it hails from the home of YOUR people."

With those words, she sent a magical blast of sunlight from palms.

Matthew burst into a shower of dark gray balls before unifying again as one thick-headed orderly. The odor of burnt flesh rose in the air.

"Gonna wish you hadn't done that." Matthew launched himself at her.

Geraldine shuffled back, her shoulders bumping the window's sill. Matthew crashed onto the twin bed and pushed himself up, scurrying backward to his feet. Fists pounding the air, he came for her again. Determination shone in the sweaty gloss on his face.

She sidestepped his punch and whirled with a double fisted magical slam of her own directly into his belly. It sent Matthew crashing to the concrete floor.

He yelped, and held his stomach as he tried to stand. The door banged open. Rod and two other orderlies came in with hesitant steps. Their faces registered their concern. Rod looked from Matthew to her and then back to him. Disbelief spoiled his features.

"Don't just stand there. Tie her up! She's gotta weapon!" Matthew shouted, his face flushed from pain.

The two men moved to restrain her.

"If you're going to lie, be good at it. Otherwise, I get bored." Geraldine held her arms high in surrender, the stance of peace and protest.

"Wait!" Rod shouted to the others. He avoided her gaze. "She ain't got a weapon. Uh, Matt must be mixed up. You know, confused. Help 'im up and let's get outta here before the doctor come 'round. Almost time for group, anyway."

Matthew cursed. "Do what I tell you. Restrain her!"

Geraldine kept her hands high, but glanced over to the corner, where the demons had been. Now, only golden light remained.

Rod shook his head. "What happened? Weapons ain't allowed and she didn't have one when I came in."

Matthew scowled at him and the other orderlies.

Seconds felt like years before Matthew answered.

"Nothin'." He yanked his shirt down, over his belly, with an angry glare at Geraldine.

"Let's go." Rod waved them out of the room.

The men obeyed. When Matthew moved his hand, Geraldine saw the burnt edges of his clothing and the blistered flesh of his abdomen.

After the other three men filed out of her room in hushed silence, Rod cast a glance back at her before slamming the door shut. The lock scraped as it slid into place, signaling the end of the test.

Today, she'd won.

"People are capable of such horrific acts." Geraldine said to herself as she climbed onto her bed. Thick blankets and a bright yellow comforter materialized beneath her body. Fluffy and soft, it cushioned her now aching limbs.

Kat meowed in obvious agreement from her spot on the hardwood floor. Polished honey brown wood gleamed in the light.

"Come on up." Geraldine patted the bed beside her.

Kat leapt onto the mounds of blankets. Once she found a spot, she lay beside Geraldine, a regal Egyptian cat, her green eyes peering across all she surveyed.

As the late morning's sunbeams brightened the room, her blinds reappeared, cloaking the thick scarred metal bars along the institution windows. Ferns flourished once more from their potted locations along the top of her bookshelves.

With Kat's purring warmth nestled next to her, Geraldine lay back and closed her eyes.

Her shadows vanquished.

For now.

To read more about this author visit the Author Spotlight.

SHE WONDERS WHILE SHE WAITS

ADRIENNE WALLACE | 1746 WORDS

She's poisonous but less dangerous than she wants to be. Her venom sporadic in it's veracity, lacks range but not commitment. She's shorter than she wants to be, but they can still hear her when she screams.

She leans forward to hoist the child by the space where arms become shoulders and successfully drags the child to her feet. She winds her fingers in between those of the child's and uses her arm muscles to push fingertip to finger webbing. The child spins in delight. They both throw their heads backwards in laughter. Their laughs last beyond their sonic energy sending waves of joy throughout the house. It's winter but everyone feels warm. Soon doors open and their mothers and siblings come to hear them laugh. They are exponentially more when they are together.

She carefully picks her poison choosing words that leave seeping holes in skin, but never for her precious niece. She saves her smiles for her. Their good is better than her bad, almost. She caves and brings her niece, the child, little pieces of joy that the child only needs because castles crumble around her. Her muscles ache from constantly trying to reconstruct the outer walls in order to protect the child. Her hurt and the potency of her poison are directly proportionate in strength. She has her sister to thanks for that.

Her sister is her hurt. Her constant, chronic hurt. Her sister is her hurt.

Mama's skin is forged from iron but soft as silk. Mama's eyes have seen signs distinguishing water fountains and train cars. Mama's eyes carry caution on top of wisdom causing their deepening and ensuring their symmetry. Her mouth speaks waterfalls of kindness and love. Mama is the most complete and the most loving. Scorpions and snakes contort into smiles when she crosses their path, her love reorienting nature. She's a shark. She's a shark that seeks hope like blood in the water. She will always be the perfect hunter. She uses her finger to draw circles and by listening she makes other people strong.

The child wants to cut away the front of her aunt's ankle and there build herself a home. She takes most of her steps besides her aunt who seems bigger than the universe. Her aunt is the sum total of all the dust of all the stars that have or that ever will exist. She lifts her aunt's arm and nuzzles into her rib cage, wishing torsos would grow together.

She prepares for the first day of her junior year of high school. She's carefree in her preparations as she already feels ascendant. She waits excitedly for the child to wake. The child knocks gently on her door and jumps into her arms when it's opened. They spin and they spin and they spin. Though she hates that her sister has moved back into her childhood quarters and brought her four children, she lives this moment live rather than in pictures. Her niece starts school on that day and moves into herself accordingly. So far, today is the best day.

The child is strong and likes to dance. She sings beautifully and constantly. She feels taller given her outsized accomplishments. She can prepare dinner for the other children while smiling and ensure they've brushed their teeth while posing for pictures. She spins in the heavy tornado of half-truths and loves her mother. Two truths and a lie, two lies and one truth, all lies, are the games she plays with her mother and comes to love. The child's brain cells fire lightning and she tries to quiet them by dancing harder.

The child packs lunches for the other children then wakes them for school. The child's tiredness chronic, she notices peers with more energy and wonders how. She is more quiet then she'd like to be and stumbles over what to say. She erases the traces she can. She straightens her hair without remorse, elongates her neck when she walks and masters the Queen's English.

The child is always in love with some worthless boy who only glances at her sideways. Still, she's married to their low-level, dingy happiness. When the boys look away she bleeds and longingly licks the tip of semi sharp kitchen knives. She relishes the stares she solicits from men; those are her favorite. She can only smile when she feels seen. Her aunt never smiles at her anymore. They have fallen out of love.

Selfies are the child's weapon of choice, her armor for a mother married to her bed. She is both a parent and a rebellious teenager. She punishes herself because of the impossibility of existing as both. She angles her hips so the lens cannot capture her scars. She presses send so she will see his sideways glances tomorrow.

Her aunt intercepts the message and comes over. Her aunt considers rousing the mother but fears the stench of the breath of futility. The aunt runs towards the child and rips her phone from her hand. She holds onto the child's wrists and sees her scars. She falls to the child's bedside and weeps for her. The child's eyes are filled with daggers.

She looks into the sun for a moment and the child is 7 then 15 years old. She pulls time backwards in vain recounting the story of the child's birth. The widening of the child shoulders causes her hands to cramp into little octopi. She doesn't let the child see her wince as she hugs her. Her wrists can't yet breathe in their new fragility

The child wonders less than she should, though she's a wanderer. When the child dances it strained– like a willow tree resisting the wind hell bent on breaking it. The child's mother is her hurt. The child's neural elasticity is her lake – to bathe, to soothe herself in and to imagine a life in which she is the counter narrative and the author. The child's imagination is shortsighted and stunted, so she punishes herself.

The child accepts affection from those who give it transactionally and bends, almost to breaking when it's given with authenticity. When her aunt is around, she feels outsized and so both strong and powerful, but also wild and uncontrollable. The child loves her aunt as much as she can and she can until she finds another boy who wants her warmth.

The child's mother and the mama's daughter is her sister. Her sister is all of their hurt.

Her sister is alone and naked trembling in the dark. Except she's long been in the light but has her eyes closed. Her sister is defensive and indefensible and can't grasp the irony. She's nearly as wide as she is tall and can't even approach the border wall of self-love and acceptance without self emulating. So she dates them. A collection of them. Slugs and sloths whose pale skin give them both a sense of self righteousness and an invisible sexiness. They are lettuce, watercress and sadness without the anger. They are nothing– but her sister feels like something when she is with them. She critiques them every once in a while hoping her sister will tilt her chin forward and look at herself. She sees the same wanting dimmed eyes in the sister's daughter and looks to the sky to invert the tears.

The child renounces her mother with an open hand slap. The child winces and begins to pick pieces of other mothers. The child cuts a large part of the glistening skin of her aunt and wraps it in a napkin. She puts the napkin in her pocket. The child asks more questions.

She fantasizes about drowning the child in her own humors. She is terrified by the way love consumes, strips her and tears off skin from the bottom of her feet. Still, she is relentless in pursuit of the child's future. Who knew love could feel like misplaced desperation?

The child is restless. Restless in her fantasizing too. The child waits while she wonders and wonders while she waits. The child would cut off her ear if she didn't deeply yearn for symmetry. The child shies from the mundane and digs deeply to find what's clearly on the surface. She fears the depths but lives within them. Her personal isn't personal.

One can simultaneously be lost and found when in the dark. The child reveled in it. Dark lipstick, dreams of dark ancestors, dark thoughts, leaden, deep reddened wrists. The child drinks the blood of serpents to make hers fade further into the deep redness of the ineptitude of her parents. She is alone and terrified of the loneliness.

She has learned to celebrate the small victories. She removes more of her skin and wraps it in wax paper. She places the package of skin on a towel in the passenger seat of her little white coupe. She waits for the child to come claim her gift. The child sleeps hopefully dreaming only of lightning. She squints her eyes to interrupt the child's dreams but asleep the child remains. She slams the car door but tiptoes to the child's bedside. "What are her wildest dreams?" she wonders. Though she has an answer, the child doesn't yet know. The child turns to her aunt and asks "why do you choose to love me?"

Her package of skin spoils whilst she tries to rouse the child. She doesn't have enough space to house the child in her own skin so she only takes in bits and pieces. She slides her hands underneath the child's arms and pulls her close; "it's time for you to grow" she whispers in the child's ear. The child tries to maintain her sleep bound retreat.

She's lucky and thus doesn't understand alternate realities like those the child dreams of. Her parents were alien in their love for her. Her father never missed a game. Not once ever. When he coached her, he saw it. She was untamable, recklessly and woefully untamable. It's what her parents most loved and feared about her.

She finally got the child to walk to the car. She blew affirmations from baby daffodils and growled simultaneously. The child's hatred blossomed in yellow but she walked, she moved, she went forward. Thank you is absent, but for now, possibility is not. She prepares another package of skin, this time with a smile.

To read more about this author visit the Author Spotlight.

II

AUTHOR INTERVIEWS

INTERVIEW WITH TONYA JONES

What was your inspiration for this story?

It's a story I started a long time ago and kind of forgot about it. I recently found it while cleaning up. I decided to rework the story. It actually was a pretty generic tale of a woman attending her friend's funeral, but then I thought it might be interesting to add a supernatural element to it. I've been wanting to do more supernatural writing... so this story gave me a chance to dabble in that.

Why did you choose a black woman for your main character?

I always write from a Black woman's perspective. It's more comfortable for me being that I am a black woman....and while I can't speak for all black women/experiences, I have a general idea what's it like to be a black woman in this society.

Why did you want to submit to Black Girl Magic Lit Magazine?

I've been wanting to submit a story for a long time, but I would always miss the deadline! I think the concept of the magazine is great and a wonderful opportunity for writers of color to create stories with lead black women characters.

What are your favorite novels or short stories and why?

It's been hard for me to sit down and read a good book since having my little one last year. However, I recently read "Ghost Summer Stories" by horror writer Tananarive Due and thoroughly enjoyed it. She's inspired me to be a better writer...to create memorable stories for readers. She's one of my favorite writers along with Octavia Butler, Toni Morrison, and the other greats of course.

Tell us something about your future writing projects.

My goal this year was to dedicate more time to writing short stories/fiction. I have so many ideas swimming in my head. I have been trying to stay committed to my goal by submitting to magazines, etc. I am also co-founder/part of a women of color (WOC) zine making group based in Portland, Oregon. The zine is called "Women of Color: How to Live in the

City of Roses and Avoid the Pricks." It's all about living as WOC in a predominately white city. The zine continues comics, poems, etc. We recently released our 12th issue.

Where can we find you online?

https://seemeblackfeministthought.wordpress.com/

Twitter: @tonyajseeme

INTERVIEW WITH MELODY KAY

What was your inspiration for this story?
This story is the culmination of everything I've learned
about dating in the last three years. I had a lot of moments
when I wanted to go back in time and change the way I
behaved or reacted to a particular guy based upon what I
know now. That's where the idea came from. What if there
was a way to go back? What if we had an opportunity to go
behind every closed door in our pasts and see the exact
reason why it didn't work out?
I was also inspired by my own need to process the disap-
pointment and discouragement that comes with romantic
rejection. It's terrible. It's one of the most damaging and
painful life experiences a person could have. And everyone
doesn't go through it. Some people are lucky and they
haven't been single since the 8th grade. They married their

college sweetheart or whatever. I think those people have no idea what rejection is really like.

I wanted to write about how much it sucks to be the girl that doesn't get the guy no matter what she does, no matter how hard she tries. Moving on is an incredibly difficult process. For sensitive people like me it takes a long time to let go. Sometimes dating hurts and I felt like it was time to write about it.

Why did you choose a black woman for your main character?

I chose 2 black women because I wanted to represent both sides of the single black woman coin. Faith is the black woman who is single and hates it. She doesn't want to be alone and she's willing to go to extreme lengths to have and keep a man. Faith is fighting her singleness every step of the way. Kim is the black woman who is single and she's okay with it. But she still has her doubts and her fears. Kim doesn't want to be desperate like Faith. She really doesn't want to play into that sad single black woman stereotype. It's still on her mind though. The difference is that she's not willing to chase or coerce a man. She has no desire to go to extreme lengths for a relationship despite wanting one very much.

Why did you want to submit to Black Girl Magic Lit Magazine?

I was excited about this magazine from the first time I heard about it. I knew I was going to submit eventually I just didn't know what I wanted to submit until I wrote this.

What are your favorite novels or short stories and why?

My favorite novel is actually a play: *A Raisin In The Sun*. I was Beneatha the first time I read it for a high school English class and I've loved it ever since. It showed me that black people can have engaging, intelligent stories written about them that don't fall under the tragedy porn umbrella. It's a dark story and there is some tragedy, but it ends with so much hope. Those are the black stories I live for.

Tell us something about your future writing projects.

I'm working with a YA author in the Writing In The Margins Mentorship Program. She's helping me revise my YA urban fantasy book. My goal is to get into traditional publishing with this project and hopefully write more books after that. I'm so excited about the possibilities right now.

Where can we find you online?

Twitter: @melody_gordon

INTERVIEW WITH NICOLE GIVENS KURTZ

What was your inspiration for this story?
The recent events of black women being harmed and killed
by police influenced "Sunshine." So many of these events
happen during the day, with people around. It felt like a
prison is around black women every where we go, but
because we're magical, we still rise. We make flowers bloom
from concrete. That's our magic.

**Why did you choose a black woman for your
main character?**
I'm a black woman, so many of my stories start people of
color. As I said earlier, "Sunshine," is about the prison (in the
story a real one), that encases my protagonist, but it's an
analogy for the real one that exists around black women and
girls in real life.

Why did you want to submit to Black Girl Magic Lit Magazine?

I submitted because the mission of promoting and spotlighting works by black authors with black characters appeals to me and is necessary.

What are your favorite novels or short stories and why?

Frankenstein is my favorite novel, because it's the ultimate conversation about white male hubris, and the horrible ramifications it causes.

Tell us something about your future writing projects.

The next novel in my Cybil Lewis series will be available in November!

Where can we find you online?

http://www.nicolegivenskurtz.com
Twitter: @nicolegkurtz
http://www.facebook.com/nicolegkurtz

INTERVIEW WITH ADRIENNE WALLACE

What was your inspiration for this story?

Honestly, my nieces inspire me to write stories about and for them. This story is about a significant turning point in my older niece's life - one in which I was lucky enough to play a part.

Why did you choose a black woman for your main character?

Black women are the main characters - in my life and as driving forces in the course of history. Anyone who doesn't have a black woman as a main character - is telling a lie. Black women have put in the blood, sweat, ingenuity, rhythm and grace that make it possible for some folks to leave easy lives. We've been left out as contributors for way too long.

Why did you want to submit to Black Girl Magic Lit Magazine?

I love black women and black women are everything.

What are your favorite novels or short stories and why?

My favorite book is *Sula* by Toni Morrison. I learn something new each and every time I read it. The Bluest Eye is also clutch. I still think about the characters in that book almost daily even though I haven't read it in years.

Tell us something about your future writing projects.

I just finished a middle grade novel which I'm shopping to agents and am editing a chapter book series that centers on an 9 year old black girl and her little brother!

Where can we find you online?

http://blackgirlmediamagic.com/adrienne-wallace-author/

Twitter: @msadriennekirk

III

BOOK EXCERPT

CERECE RENNIE MURPHY | TO
FIND YOU

IN THE BEGINNING

1754 ~ Gold Coast, Ghana

I wait for him here at the place where the night sky and the earth become lovers. In the tall grass of our homeland, between two kingdoms, we meet.

Getting here early is easier than slipping away late, especially now when life in my village is bustling with the preparations for our wedding in just three days.

But as the reeds lick the backs of my calves, I know that this is only one part of the reason I wait.

The truth is that I like to feel him coming. At this hour,

when my imagination reigns over every shape and whisper, I can almost see him walking on limbs taller and stronger than mine will ever be. He cuts through the night that hides his slightly lighter shade and stalks his prey. I cannot hear his approach, but I feel him drawing near, compelled by the same force that holds me where I stand--the scent of my desire in the air.

I close my eyes and breathe deeply, imagining I can taste him, too. The flavor is salt, sweet grass, and home. It fills my senses and makes me thirsty.

On the outside, my knees shake and my heart pounds, impatient for its mate, while the deepest part of me grows calm and still--stretching towards the peace that only his presence brings.

And he's close now, so close.

W hen we were children, Ekow was such a scrawny thing. I used to like to wrestle him just to beat him, just to prove that I could. I was young, determined and more than a little jealous of the physical prowess of my older brothers. Secretly, I wanted to be like them, but my youngest brother, Kofi, was already 10 years my senior by the time I could walk. With Ekow, I knew I'd finally found a way to prove that no boy could match me.

My laughter rumbles in the stillness as I think of it. Oh, how angry he would be every time I beat him! And in the beginning, there were many, many times when I did. He would get so angry that his ears would twitch. He would stomp away from his defeat with his hands balled up in knobby little fists--eyes glaring, ears twitching, while one of our elders cackled nearby with me sticking out my tongue. We didn't see each other often enough for me to beat him every day, but I looked forward to it whenever I could. I was always stronger than I looked, and even when he grew a little taller than me, his limbs seemed to flail awkwardly about him so that he was never quite coordinated. And in my delicious reign as his tormentor, time seemed to stretch on forever, until one day, it stopped.

I remember the sun burned low in the sky that day as the dust and amber light conspired against me in swirling fits that stung my eyes. Rolling around on the ground, I was shocked to find myself panting for air. Suddenly, his legs overpowered me. I couldn't throw him the way I had been able to before. His grip was a vice that I had to sweat to free myself from, and even then, he could catch me again, quickly--too quickly for my liking.

Unable to break free, I grunted and cursed as he pinned me down on my back. At first, I refused to meet his gaze. Beneath my eyelashes, I could swear I saw my own taunting smirk, the same one I had given him year after year, curling the corners of his lips. Enraged, I shut my eyes and kicked my legs furiously, all to no avail. I could feel the muscles of his powerful thighs holding me in place without the slightest indication of strain, and I couldn't stand it.

As if sensing the scream that would send my brothers flying to my aid, he suddenly lifted his body from mine, then leaned over to adjust his grip so that our hands were stretched out above my head, palm to palm, fingers intertwined in the grass and the dirt beneath us.

How did I not know, even then . . . ?

Something about the gesture was so strange that it distracted me from my fury. The feel of his hands pressed firmly into mine made my stomach flutter and clench in a way that was startling, but not unpleasant.

"Ama," he called. "Ama, don't scream. Ama, please, surrender."

It must have been the "surrender" that made my eyes fly open to meet his in absolute indignation.

Sometimes I like to think that if hadn't opened my eyes, it never would have happened, but this is, of course, foolish. I was meant to see.

I looked up to find him staring down at me. The smirk I'd feared was nowhere in sight.

Instead, his eyes held the same wariness I felt as I looked back at him, then quickly dissolved into something else.

He eyed my mouth with what I understand now as a mixture of surprise and captivation. Back then, I still had no idea what was happening, but as his gaze lingered, I began to feel like someone was seeing me truly for the first time in my life. I remember fighting the nameless emotion that closed my throat and pricked my eyes.

"Ama, surrender," he whispered, "Please."

And that's when I understood that I held him in place as much as he held me.

"Please," he said again, and I finally realized what I needed to do all along.

Seeing the answer there in my eyes, he released my hands and rose to his feet. I remember averting my eyes against the sudden rush of loneliness that came as he left. But at the corner of my vision, I saw it, his hand extended out to help me up. He'd done it before, even as I beat him and he'd risen in defeat while I remained holding my belly in victorious laughter on the ground. I'd always ignored the gesture until that moment, when suddenly it felt like the most natural thing in the world to accept his help.

When I finally stood, I noticed for the first time that he'd grown at least 10 inches since the last time I saw him.

Despite my daze, I frowned. "You're taller than me," I said in dismay.

"No, Ama," he replied. Ekow's voice was deep and heavy as he stepped forward to take my other hand in his. "We are exactly the same height."

I was 13 years old; Ekow was 16, and after that, nothing between us was ever the same.

With my eyes closed, it takes only a moment for him to close the distance. His hands cover my shoulders as his lips trace the curve of my neck. This is our greeting. No words. We speak in action.

I let my head fall back against his chest and feel his smile press into my skin at the place where my hum echoes deepest. He knows it is a sound I make only for him. When I turn to face him, I need no invitation. I wrap both hands around his neck and pull him closer, touching his lips to mine gently, to feel their full weight and softness. It is a chaste kiss, though I don't know why I do this. There is nothing chaste about why we are here. We are as ravenous as love itself, but I always feel the need to honor this power between us before we are consumed.

But one thing always leads to another, and as I pull him closer, lifting my chest to his, reverence gives way to something else entirely.

He lifts me in one quick motion onto him then lowers me down to the ground on his lap. We are a frenzy of arms and kisses, tongues tasting, teeth nibbling, and skin yearning to be closer still. His hands are in my hair, kneading my scalp as his kiss deepens. My mouth and my legs open wider in unison. Tears sting my eyes with every sensation I feel. I want to cry and laugh and scream. But the release is like the edge of a precipice I don't know how to jump off of, and so I choose to move instead, rocking against him slowly.

His eyes are open now as he kisses me, watching my mood, reading my signs. Caressing my back his fingers move up and down my spine, loosening, unfastening, until I am naked in his lap. I look down in surprise to find that he is too.

My expression makes him chuckle with pride, knowing and devilish. And if it wasn't for the same power that I have over him, I would be terrified to be so taken with him. Because, in moments like this, the love I feel is so overwhelming that I'm sure the need to give it will break me in two.

How can I love one person this much and survive?

As Ekow lays our bodies down, I find myself sucked into the silence between death and creation. The fear slips between us like a foreign substance, threatening to cut the very fabric of which we are made, but Ekow will have none of it. With a heart that knows me, and steady, faithful hands, he reaches into the darkness and pulls me back.

Shaking his head, he takes my hand and kisses each finger before bringing them to his chest.

"It's just us, Ama. It's just us."

And I know it again, as always. My tears release the weight of silence as something new is born and an even deeper love takes its first breath. I watch him wait as the tide of my emotions recede enough for me to breathe and expand.

The lightness of it makes me smile. From his questioning eyes, I know that he doesn't quite understand what's happened, but it only takes a moment for me to show him. I pull him into my kiss and pour everything that I know, everything that I am into it. Above me, he's breathless, enchanted by the ferocity of my caress.

I pull him closer still and feel the weight of him pressing at my opening. Large and insistent. Yet, he lingers.

It drives me crazy.

The muscles in my thighs twitch and tremble with desire. Vaguely, I recall that I'm not supposed to open so readily. Auntie says I should tease a man, make him beg for my sweetness, but I no longer care. There is no room for pretense between us and his eyes tell me it wouldn't matter anyway.

He knows what is his.

I squirm underneath him anxiously--half desperate, half greedy, and all in a rush, but he holds me still with the weight of his body as he slowly pushes inside.

And whatever feeling I had, whatever thought was racing, becomes silent. My whole being becomes focused on the path he is taking. I close my eyes and feel--wanting more, wanting everything all at once.

"Open your eyes. Look at me, Ama."

I struggle to find the focus to do what he asks, but then his hand comes up to rest on my forehead. I feel his thumb gently stroking my hairline as the heat from his touch settles into my skin. My eyes open to find that he is cradling me from my head to the very tips of my toes, from the inside out he surrounds me.

I find his eyes and I can't help returning the wonder and joy that I see in them.

I will never be as safe as I am now. The realization makes the air itself burn in my throat as my tears begin to swell.

He holds us still as time hovers, just allowing us to feel.

It is perfect, until I let out a shuddering breath that seems to weaken his resolve. He presses his forehead to mine and kisses me deeper, harder and then we start to move. And there is nothing and no one else who could reach me in this moment. I surrender to him as he surrenders to me--affirming that we are one being in the world that we create.

There is nothing quick or rushed in how he moves over me. It is not always like this when we come together, but tonight he savors every stroke and makes me do the same. Our legs twist and intertwine with the slim reeds of grass that bend into our makeshift bed and dance in the cool breeze around us. He keeps my head in his palm while seeking out my fingers with his other hand. With our palms pressed together, fingers intertwined, I fall deeper in love with every second that passes.

Though our marriage ceremony has yet to be, I know we have loved each other from the beginning of forever. The thought makes my hips rise in celebration. In response, he spreads me wider, presses deeper until I'm quivering, incoherent bliss.

His kisses flutter at the edge of my skin, but I feel them deep in my bones. He's whispering something to me that I sense more than hear. He is professing what I already know, have always known.

He loves me

As I love him.

I say the words back to him though there is no need. We witness to the Spirits, the air between us, and the beckoning light that tells us that it is time for us to part.

He holds me tight enough to feel it long after he's gone before disappearing into the brush. His quick feet are light against the ground as he runs, but I can still hear the sounds of his joy, hooting and howling at the dawn. There's no need to be quiet. He's already late for the morning fishing, and with the grin he'll surely be wearing when he gets there, it won't be hard for his brothers to guess why.

As I walk back to the place that will only be my home for a little longer, I'm sure that everything must be right with the world for him to be with me and me with him. So perfect. His presence lingers deliciously in the ache of my limbs and the smell of him on my skin. The thought makes me smile as I look forward to everything our life together will bring. So lost was I in my daydreams, that I was completely unprepared for the sight of what was to come when I returned to my village.

But I should have known. If I was not so lost, I would have caught the foul stench of burning flesh.

© 2016 by Cerece Rennie Murphy

Cerece Rennie Murphy first fell in love with science fiction watching *Empire Strikes Back* at the Uptown Theater in Washington, DC with her sister and mother. It's a love affair that has grown ever since.

In addition to working on the release of the 2nd book in the Ellis and The Magic Mirror children's book series with her son, as well as a time-bending romance, Mrs. Murphy is developing a 2-part science fiction thriller set in outer space. Mrs. Murphy lives and writes in her hometown of Washington, DC with her husband, two children and the family dog, Yoda. To learn more about the author and her upcoming projects, please visit her website at www.cerecerenniemurphy.com.

To Find You will be released in paperback and ebook on

November 29, 2016

Pre-Order Your Copy on Amazon, Barnes and Noble, or visit www.cerecerenniemurphy.com

IV

AUTHOR INTERVIEW

AUTHOR INTERVIEW | CHANEL HARRY

Chanel Harry, author of the new horror novel *Skin Witch* agreed to "sit down" with us and give us an interview to tell us about her latest project and what she has coming down the pike.

Chanel, can you give us a Short Bio?
I live in the Bronx, but lived a lot of places. So I'd like to say that I am from all over the East Coast.
I've been into all things horror and sci-fi since I was about five years old with Tales From The Crypt: Demon Knight being one of the first movies that have made an impact on my already developing writer brain. I have always loved reading and writing and have written stories since I could remember.
I have written two novels so far, one is about a Trinidadian

(My maternal heritage) vampire called the Soucouyant. That novel is called *Skin Witch*. I have also written that as three novellas in one.

Heebie Jeebies: Tales of Terror is my second bad ass anthology book. It has such depraved stories that I have written, that even I would get scared and nothing scares me lol.

Amazon's synopsis for *Skin Witch* states: Soucouyants are legendary witch vampires that hail from the sister islands of Trinidad and Tobago. They are seductive women who live a normal existence by day but at night, shed their skin to turn into a supernatural ball of fire to feast on the blood of the living. Although only perceived as creatures of West Indian folklore, they are very much real and hunger to tell their stories. Follow three, beautiful soucouyants as they each tell their tales of obeah, love, revenge, and murder. Can you give us a synopsis of each of the three soucouyants' stories in Skin Witch?

There are three stories in Skin Witch. The first story, "Birth" is about the very first Soucouyant to ever live in Trinidad and Tobago. This story is set during the dark colonial slave period in Trinidad where a young slave girl unlocks her Soucouyant powers after her abuse from her slave master and his daughter.

The second story, "Bloodlines" is set in modern day Trinidad and it involves a woman who is an art teacher by day and a deadly Soucouyant by night. She lives this way until the superstitious locals hire a Soucouyant hunter. Now she must find out who that hunter is before it's too late.

The third and final story, "The Secret" is set in modern day Tobago (the sister isle to Trinidad.) This story is told through two different perspectives; a man and a Soucouyant. A young man from America moves back to Tobago after his parents' death, inherits his father's restaurants. Little does he know that a beautiful woman is seeking revenge against him and his family with a secret of her own.

What was your inspiration for your project, why pull from the Trinidad & Tobago traditions of Soucouyants?

The inspiration for this book was from my own heritage. I was always hearing about the horrifying legend of the Soucouyant since I could remember. My mother is a native of Trinidad and Tobago so I wanted to pull from my heritage and bring the story of the Soucouyant to America and to Americans.

How do you feel being a POC creator?

There were some barriers that I faced once I finished this

book, being a POC creator and that was a lot of POC that I knew of really [didn't] support me. However, when I joined other POC book groups of my genre they out right supported this book!

Personally, I feel that POC becoming indie authors is GREAT! We get to write what we want how we want! We don't have to change to fit a "mass audience" because thanks to social media, we can get our right audience in our respective genres.

I would change one thing about the process to get my project finished and that would be better deadlines for myself!

What do you think POC creators need to succeed?

I think we need grassroots support first then everything will unfold!

What was the easiest thing about getting your novel to the finish line? The hardest?

The easiest thing about getting my novel to the finish line was writing it! I enjoy typing so writing everyday isn't an issue for me. However, the hardest was finding time to edit it but I looked into hiring a freelance editor to help me along the way!

Tell us something about your future projects.

Well, I have a horror anthology that I will be writing by myself called *Heebie Jeebies: Tales of Terror* that I am excited to release on Halloween. I also will be writing a science fiction Trilogy called Reverse Kingdom that I am so in love with! I can't wait for my readers to read those!

What are your favorite novels or short stories and why?

My favorite novel(s) would be "Carrie" by Stephen King. That one is my favorite because I went through a lot of bullying as a kid and not only was because that book was a horror book but because it gave me strength to go to school and face my tormentors every day. My most second favorite novel is "Interview with The Vampire" by Anne Rice. Reason being is I love vampires and I just love the way that she writes them so beautifully.

What does Black Girl Magic mean to you?

Wow, Black Girl Magic to me means that we as black girls/women have our own power that's hidden within us no matter how big or small it is. We have potential and wonderment inside of us that we can unlock!

If you'd like to purchase Skin Witch it is available on Amazon right now!

If you'd like to connect with Chanel, you can get up with her through her website & social media:
http://authorchanelharry.wix.com/authorchanelharry
https://www.facebook.com/chanel.m.harry

THANK YOU

If you'd like to be the first to learn about Black Girl Magic
Lit Mag news you can join our Mailing List & read story
excerpts and read book reviews on our site at
http://www.blackgirlmagicmag.com

We accept story submissions on a quarterly basis. If you're
interested in submitting please check our website for
guidelines.

We'd also love to connect with you on Twitter & Facebook.

**YOU CAN PURCHASE PAST & FUTURE ISSUES ON
AMAZON**

Made in the USA
Middletown, DE
11 August 2022

71120212R00060